To Ella
all my lov~
Nann~

D1277624

The Wit and Wisdom of
Cats & Kittens

This is a STAR FIRE book

STAR FIRE BOOKS
Crabtree Hall, Crabtree Lane
Fulham, London SW6 6TY
United Kingdom

www.star-fire.co.uk

First published 2008

09 11 10 08

3 5 7 9 10 8 6 4

Star Fire is part of The Foundry Creative Media Company Limited

The CIP record for this book is available from the British Library.

ISBN: 978 1 84451 808 1

Printed in China

Thanks to: Cat Emslie, Andy Frostick, Sara Robson,
Gemma Walters and Nick Wells

The Wit and Wisdom of Cats & Kittens

Ulysses Brave

STAR FIRE

I am seeing
my tail's path

Foreword

For years I studied Zen and the Art of
Animal Self-consciousness. Subsequently I
have written a large number of management,
self-help and philosophical texts over the
years, which have provided helpful advice
to those less fortunate than myself.
Here then, is my latest offering.

Ulysses Brave

Try to keep in touch with your inner self. Focus on an object close by, perhaps a candle, breath in and slowly feed your breath out through your solar plexus.

*It is always useful to find
a moment to appreciate
the delicate beauty of the
natural world.*

Smother love is often about the giver rather than the receiver. To avoid causing offence, try to think about something that makes you really happy.

When receiving unexpected news, try not to betray your true feelings until the full implications become apparent.

Small children can be startled
by the most mundane of
noises. A car door from a
distance can sound like the
sky falling down when heard
for the very first time.

Always find time to pamper yourself.

You can kid some of the people some of the time, but never try to kid yourself.

Sometimes 599 TV channels simply don't provide enough entertainment. Try to seek within yourself.

For those who suffer from paranoia, always check to make sure that the sky is not going to fall down, before embarking on a long journey.

Visit your doctor regularly.

Inner beauty lasts longer
than the more obvious
seductions, so throw away
the miniskirt and
thigh-length boots.

As you grow older, keeping warm becomes more important than looking good.

If you're in a rut, try taking a new perspective on life: wear different clothes to work, change your hair, stare into a new corner of the room.

Making friendships outside your immediate community will bring fresh perspectives on life. It is always more difficult to eat a friend.

Pointless competitions can be
useful in relieving stress.

Stay alert at all times, alert to any opportunity for rest.

*Of course, fruit and
vegetables are good for you,
but they are also an excellent
source of shade.*

If someone wants to fight,
it is impolite to ignore them.

Life often presents you with difficult choices. But who made up the rules? Why choose at all?

*Waiting without anxiety is
one of life's great skills.
Practise every day on the
way to work or school.*

Too much love can crush you. Try to take regular breaks.

*Dieting can have
unfortunate consequences
for your mental well-being.*

Treat each other with respect, even if other people can only look at the colour of your eyes.

*Endless games of cat
and mouse will dull your
emotional responses.*

Be wary of false gods. Too much adoration can turn you into a statuesque caricature of yourself.

Try to find friends
amongst those you do
not wish to eat.

*If you are embarrassed
by your actions, try hiding
from yourself.*

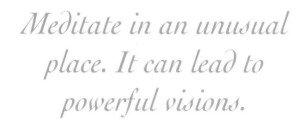

Meditate in an unusual place. It can lead to powerful visions.

When faced with the unexpected,
try to remain calm and take
control of events.

At around lunchtime, don't forget to check the sky again.

Your stressful life demands that you take less sleep than you need. Try to compensate whenever you can.

*Always study the eyes of
your opponent. Sometimes,
they might just be hungry.*

Don't be afraid of your appearance. Others might be colour blind.

See you again...